Joy

A Spiritual

Way of Life

Christine A. Adams

Copyright

Paperback ISBN: 979-83076067-0-4

First paperback edition January 2025

Edited by MD Hanley

Word Cloud Art Designed by MD Hanley

Cover photography by Harrison Hanley

Page 33 photo credit to Bernie Murphy

https://www.harrywander.com/

Graphics by https://www.wordclouds.com/

Hanley-Adams Publishing

Boxboro, MA 01719

www.hanleyadamspublishing.com

Foreword

Seeking a spiritual life is the first step to a more joyful life. We might think people, or things, will make us happy but that is only a "fleeting" happiness. Real joy cannot **come to us;** it has to **come from us.**

Once again, gratitude is the key to joy! What we believe about the world around us frames our thinking about life itself. Do you see the world with apprehension, fear, guilt, anger, remorse or with love, gratitude and appreciation? Are you thankful to the Almighty Creator who gave you life in this world? Joy comes when we **reframe** life situations more positively and create our joy from within our soul.

Look to nature! Look to the majesty and the miracle of healing within you. To the joyous miracle of life around you and within you. Watch the seasons change. Notice the ongoing birth/rebirth cycle of life in the birth of a child. All moments of birth are the promise of the extension of creation, and of eternal joy.

God created you for a purpose! You are a child of God! His will for you is joy!

Let God speak to you as a loving parent. Stop bombarding your mind with negative thoughts. Let your worries, anxiety and fears go to God. Use self reflection, prayer and meditation and the reading of scriptures to bring you back to positive thoughts.

But what about death, and sickness and old age? We accept these things we cannot change and change the things we can! We can change ourselves, our behaviors, our attitude and our thinking to a more God centered place. We just need to hang on in the darkness of winter remembering that spring is on the way!

By spreading joy, we keep alive the possibility of a miracle. God speaks to us through others. Be generous by sharing your gifts with others. Let the happiness of others fill you with joy. Laugh again and again! Don't let your relationship to "machines" replace relating to people directly.

By pursuing a spiritual way of life, you will find great joy as well as the gift of love, peace and wisdom. There will be moments of spiritual awakening as well as unexpected miracles. Just know that God's will for you is joy! Through faith, you will find the promise of an eternal joy.

1.

Happiness is a choice! Nothing will make you happy until you decide to be happy. It won't come **to you** because it comes **from you.** The greatest influence in increasing happiness in any situation is our ability to **reframe** our situation more positively, our ability to experience gratitude, or our choice to be kind, generous, and loving. What we believe creates our joy!

2.

Grateful thoughts are happy thoughts. You cannot be thankful and unhappy at the same time; it's impossible. God's will for you is joy. Accept joy, and realize that everything that happens to you "good and bad" blesses you. Believe that life is good and it will be!

3.

Look to nature! There's great joy in its creation. Nothing comes from nothing, there must be a cause to have an effect. God is that "first cause of creation."

4.

You are part of the natural world! Look to the majesty and the miracle of healing within you and around you. All things functioning and changing at the same time. You are the joyous miracle of life!

5.

All things in nature serve a purpose, contributing to the greater good of all creation. Perhaps we are asked to accept that we are not the creator of all things; but that we can spread the spiritual message of creation by seeing beyond the human perspective of loss, violence and death. Could it be that the material world is full of illusions while the real world is spiritual, of God?

6.

Stop for a moment! Watch the seasons change. All things in nature change, including you and your seasons of life. Embrace these changes. God is there in the barrenness, the new beginnings, the fruitfulness, and the changing colors of life. Thank God for your life.

7.

Rejoice in the birth of a child. The secret of all happiness is in the "birth /rebirth cycle". That child may reproduce another child-and the cycle of life goes on and on! Moments of birth are the promise of the extension of creation, or everlasting life. That is eternal joy!

8.

In times of difficulty, gratitude means turning our will over to God's greater plan. Gratitude enhances the colorful canvas of our lives by allowing us to see the larger picture. How do you see the world? Are you fearful and apprehensive all the time? Is a negative attitude keeping you from any chance of a joyful connection with others? Trust God and move forward with courage.

9

The "good news" is that there's always **hope** if we look for it. The secret of the lesson of nature is one of second chances. After the darkness of night comes the dawn. Spring brings the advent of new life. Our most difficult tribulations can bring unknown blessings. Dare to imagine, to hope for the good things that may come. We're not all knowing but God is and He is watching over us and loves us. Let go and let God in good faith.

10.

Listen to your thoughts! If you say negative things like, "this job is killing me", or "she makes me sick", your mind will believe you and in time you might not feel so good. Reframe this to be positive as "I'm glad to have a job" and "I will pray for her". Ask God for help in these situations.

11.

Accept that other people, places, and things do not have the ability to make you unhappy, discontent, or agitated. Happiness is an "inside job". A choice we make every day. There's always something to be happy about, even if it is just this very moment that we share. Let's rejoice in it!

12.

Thinking negative thoughts attracts more negative Energy to you. When you are surrounded with negative Energy, you are distracted and less able to cope with the challenges of everyday living. Pay attention to your thoughts and the mental energy of the people around you, of the media and internet influences that you allow into your space. Negative thoughts can lead you to depression and despair, which will kill the joy within you. Protect your mental health every day by thinking positive thoughts.

13.

Self-reflection, prayer, meditation, and the reading of the scriptures lead to positive thoughts. "Spiritual inquiry" turns our attention toward a more spiritual view of life. Be grateful for your inquiring mind, your gift of sight, your ability to hear sounds of laughter, taste the sweetness of food, and your ability to grow and change.

14.

Love yourself! Be kind to your mind. If you're constantly bombarding your mind with disparaging thoughts like, "I can't do this", "I'm not smart enough", "I'm not pretty enough", "I will always make mistakes", "and no one will ever love me"! Tell that negative voice you are not listening to it anymore. Let God speak to you as a loving parent. God's will for you is joy. Take it!

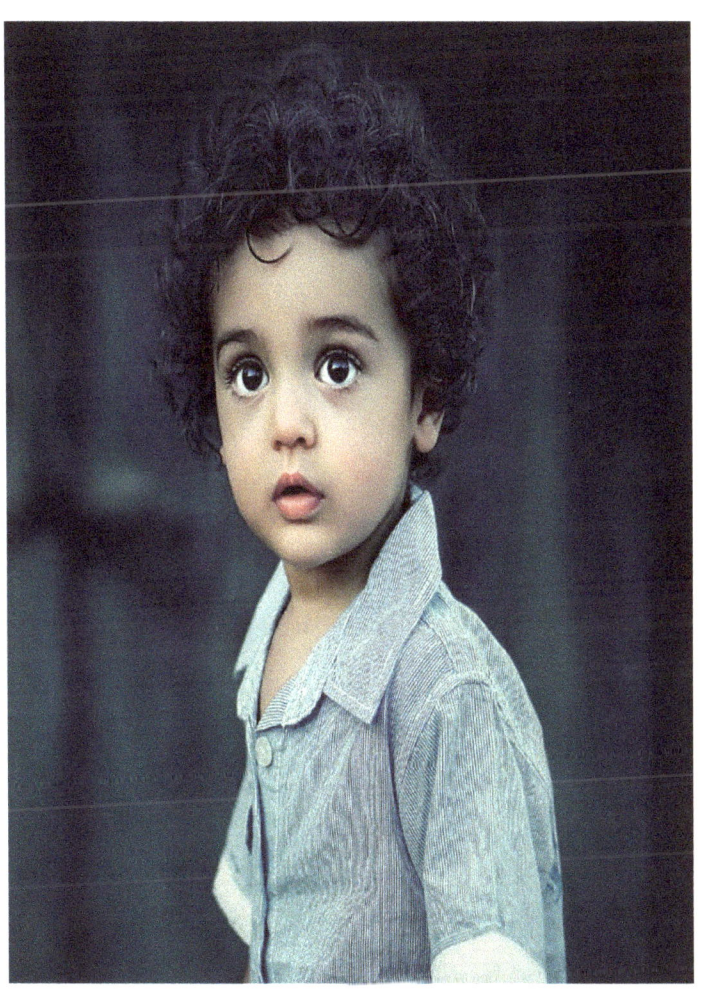

15.

When adversity comes to you, accept it by remembering that sometimes what seems negative can have unknown, positive results. We can't know the future. Therefore, we never have the whole picture. Remember, God will be protecting you along the way. Dismiss worry, anxiety, and fears by giving them to God.

16.

We find joy by caring for ourselves and others. By accepting life as it unfolds and trusting in the benevolence of God. When we reach out to help others, we are also helping ourself. This brings us a sense of knowing that we aren't alone!

17.

Our peace of mind begins within our own thoughts. We train our minds to correct ego-based distortions. It is from that peace of mind that we reframe our perspective to a more joyful place. The obstacles to peace are fear, guilt, anger, and judgment.

18.

Our fears can interrupt our peace of mind. When fear comes, we lose the present moment and our chance for real joy. Many times we are afraid of things that never happen! However, we do need a "prudent fear of harm" to help us hold back and reconsider some actions. Experience teaches us the difference between what is real and what is not.

19.

Guilty thoughts can taint our motives and color are thinking. Acting out of guilt causes us mental confusion and mental unrest. Again, it robs us of our peace of mind. When we act out of guilt, we feel compelled to act; but, we find joy when we give by our own free choice.

20.

Anger can be a stimulus for good works. We can dedicate ourselves to a purposeful cause, like fighting injustice or the inequity of life. In that sense, it can bring happiness to us. However, unresolved personal anger can steal our joy. Reframe your thinking when anger festers and dominates your thoughts. Forgive others.

21.

Forgiveness and humility can be the antidote for lingering anger. Forgiveness is tied to faith because when we refuse to forgive, we play God by rendering absolute judgments of evil, or sin, on others. We have been forgiven by God because He loves us unconditionally. Why not give that same forgiveness to others?

22.

Reframe your thinking by "letting go and letting God". When we play God, we can easily get so caught up in judging others, that we will find we are rarely happy ourselves.

23.

Forgive yourself, just as God has forgiven you. You are his child, you are exactly where you are supposed to be at this moment. Forgive others because they are also children of God.

24.

When we accept life on life's terms, we automatically find gratitude. Acceptance and gratitude are often intertwined. Gratitude brings a sense of peace, that quietness of the soul. Ultimately, gratitude attracts more blessings as we think of what God is doing for us, not what we "don't have".

25.

We start by accepting what we can't change. We can't change missed opportunities, irreversible tragedies, or the death of a loved one. Nor, are we responsible for the attitudes, behavior, or unwise choices of others. Then, of course, you can't change old age or your own mortality. You might feel mad at God, thinking you are being punished. At this time, your faith is being tested. Hang on!

26.

Find the courage to change the things you can. You can change yourself, your behavior, your habits; and most importantly, you can change your thinking. Reframe your thoughts to more positive "God centered thinking" and you will find joy!

27.

Like the seasons, our life goes from the cold months of winter, to the warmth of spring and the leisure of summer, to the fullness of fall, and back to the bleak cold again. Accept change, it only hurts when we resist it!

28.

Be open-minded! God knows more than we know about the journey we are on. There are times when an enemy becomes our greatest teacher or when the oldest, physically weakest one can direct the strongest younger ones. Keep open to the possibilities of your life and keep going in good faith.

29.

Happiness comes to those who spread joy. It's a wise man who knows this truth. The way to be happy yourself is to make those around you happy. When a situation seems hopeless, be open to the possibility of a miracle. When all seems lost, there is always hope. God can make the impossible happen for you and others. Wait for the miracle, anticipate its coming and when it does - rejoice!

30.

Parents can influence their children by emanating a positive, hopeful message in the light of any darkness; **or** harm them with judgmental messages of fears and hatred of others. A joyful leader can influence the world with messages of hope and love, while a dictator can cause fear with messages of vengeance and hatred. Spreading joy and love is the work of all God's children.

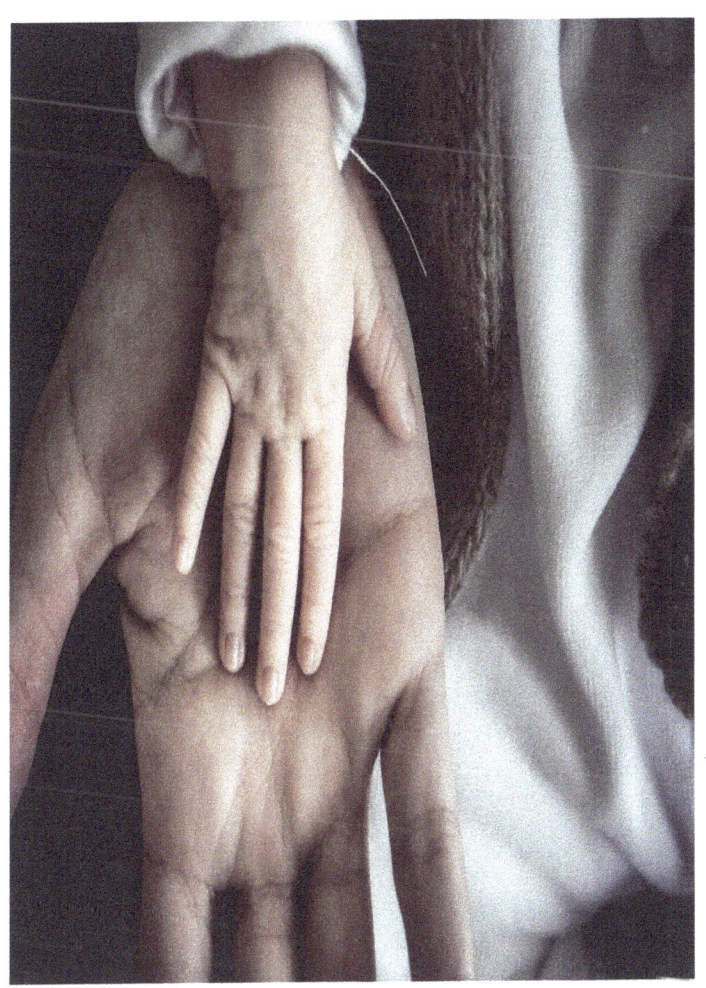

31.

To find joy, we must look **inside** ourselves paying attention to our "inner values". When we seek happiness outside ourselves through money, sex, power, big cars, and big houses, we undermine our chances for real joy. When we go inside to our very soul - to a spiritual place- we find a quiet place of communion, of belonging. Eternal Joy and Love live there,

.

32.

Material possessions do not have permanence! With ego-based materialistic thinking, we can think we are defined by our possessions, by who loves us, or by our accomplishments, or our lineage. Eventually, the "Mercedes" we buy will wear out, the house will deteriorate, and to our great sorrow, the ones we love will die. All material things are transitory!

33.

Grief is a natural process of loss and it has its own poignant joy and beauty. It's a tribute to your loved one and a reminder of the depth of the love you have known. In time only loving, happy moments will endure!

34.

Offset the seduction of modern technology! The Internet can be a necessary part of modern living; but it also can invite you to engage in a comparison of worldly goods, of lifestyles, even degrees of projected happiness. It can induce you to over consume worldly goods, be influenced by a "group mentality", all the while projecting distance, anonymity, and innocence. Protect your thoughts, protect your right to joy!

35.

Seek out togetherness, belonging, soul touching, and then you will find joy. In today's world, we are asked to put aside human relating for the sake of expediency and efficiency. Resist this trend and seek out human feelings of compassion and belonging by "soul touching" with moments of love and service. Resist superficial relating to cell phones, computers, and TV's, whenever possible.

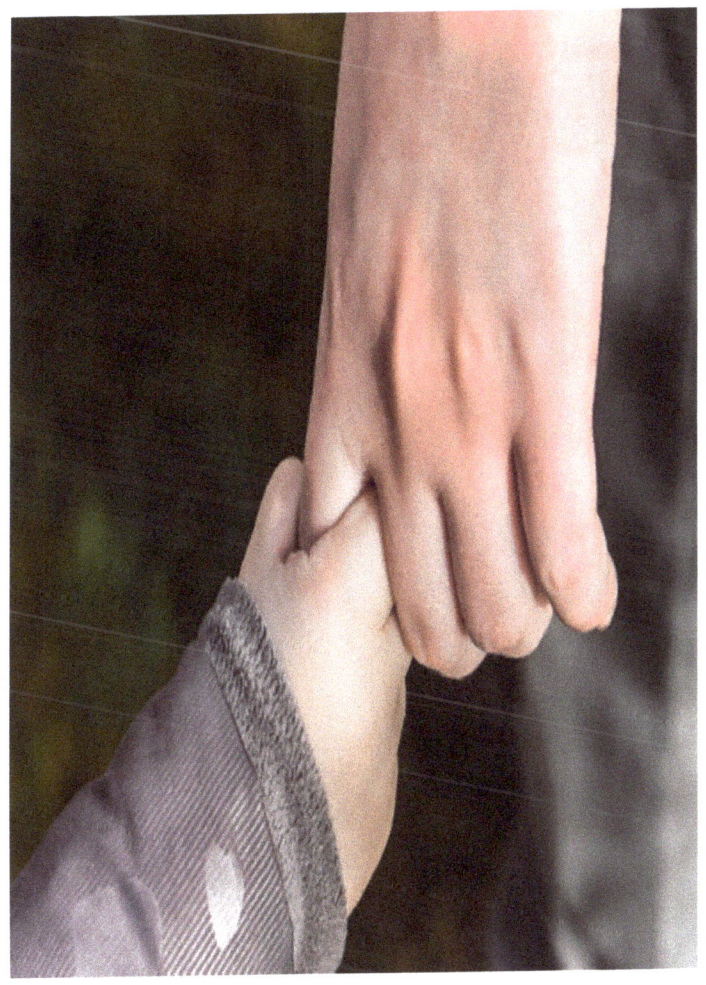

36.

God is love! He speaks to us through others. Through human contact, we know we are alive, we are loved, we have meaning! That is joyful!

37.

Human relationships are best when communication is in context. You can't feel the depth of love, or get a sense of togetherness, from an email or a text message. Words are just words without context. Face to face is the pathway to experiencing the deepest love.

38.

It doesn't matter what gifts you have, share them with others. Be generous! Let the happiness of others fill you with joy. You might be able to fix things that break, so help others to fix things. You might be good at cooking, so feed others. You might be able to make everyone laugh, do it! Don't compare yourself to others. You are unique and valuable for your own gifts.

39.

Be aware of what steals joy from you. If you can't quite define it, just remember what brings you joy. Is it the laughter of your child? Is it listening to Chopin? Is it the sound of the ocean? Is it meditation and prayer? Seek out these joyful moments - again and again!

40.

Embrace playfulness, humor. Allow yourself to have fun. Laugh out loud, laugh again and again. When you find someone who makes you laugh, hold them close! Sing, dance, or play, all lead to joy.

41.

Pursue creative endeavors - paint, build, write, garden, cook, or play music. Show little children how to express themselves through creativity. Take them beyond video games. Spread joy by helping them experience the unique sense of accomplishment as they create something of their own. God gave you the ability to create, share it!

42.

There is a "spiritual awakening" that comes to those who seek it. With this spiritual awakening comes peace and with peace comes wisdom. When we find the wisdom to live happily, to love others who are also children of God, who are seeking the same peace, there is harmony in the world. Harmony always allows room for joy!

43.

Throughout history, humanity has held onto the concept of an "afterlife". As a result, there remains a tenuous and sacred link to our departed loved ones through cherished memories, enduring love, and the strength of their undying spirit. This connection enables us to accept this loss of love and navigate the grieving process by remembering our shared experiences. It's within this connection of spirits that eternal joy resides.

44.

We may find ourselves pursuing fleeting moments of happiness in our daily lives; but really we seek an eternal serenity, or the joyful state of knowing we are loved and will **always** be protected by God. There is the promise of an eternal joy in faith. Christians believe in the connection to Christ, we can pursue a Christian life, and we will find a joy that lasts forever. The Bible tells us that Jesus said, **"So you have sorrow now, but I will see you again, your heart will rejoice and no one will take away your joy from you." John 16: 22**

45.

*Searching for a spiritual way of life is a lifelong process. It is not arduous or heavy, but joyful. It's marked with many incredible moments of spiritual awakening and many miracles. In faith, we believe that a loving God is doing for us what we cannot do for ourselves. And that God's will for us will **always** be joy!*

— *Notes* —

— Notes —

Notes

About the Author of This Book

Christine A. Adams

Christine A. Adams, M.A., has been writing about issues of addiction, relationships, spirituality, and education for over 35 years. She has over 3,000,000 separate books and pamphlets in print with works published in 54 countries translated into many languages. Christine, an English teacher, was also formerly trained as an addiction counselor in 1986. However, most of her writing parallels her life experiences. Her early writings were about the alcoholic marriage, adult children of alcoholics, teen alcoholism, and sexual addiction. Then came books about spirituality, relationships, grief therapy and education.

In addition, she has produced four very popular Elf Help children's books: <u>Happy To Be Me</u>, <u>Learning To Be A Good Friend</u>, <u>Worry, Worry, Go Away</u>, and <u>God Made Us One By One.</u> One of her best-known recovery books is the adult Elf Help gift book, <u>One Day At A Time Therapy</u> which is still selling in places like Taiwan, China, South Korea, Portugal, the Netherlands, Austria, Sweden, Indonesia, and Brazil.

Among her other books are: <u>Seasons: Spiritual Meditations for Winter, Spring, Summer, and Fall</u>; <u>Let Go, Let God</u>; <u>Teacher of God</u>; <u>Holy Relationships</u>; and <u>ABC's of Grief: A Handbook For Survivors</u>. She has also written a fictional narrative, inspired by her years of teaching, titled <u>The School Factory</u>, as well as a romantic novel named <u>September Love</u>. Additionally, she has authored four out of the five titles in the <u>Spiritual Way of Life</u> series, which encompass Joy, Peace, Love, Acceptance, and Gratitude.

Visit her at www.christineaadams.com or www.hanleyadamspublishing.com to find all her books.

Books by Christine A. Adams

Peace: A Spiritual Way of Life

Love: A Spiritual Way of Life

Acceptance: A Spiritual Way of Life

Gratitude: A Spiritual Way of Life

Seasons: Spiritual Meditations For
Winter, Spring, Summer, and Fall

Spirituality: A Life Force

ABC's of Grief – A Handbook for Survivors

Let Go and Let God

Teacher of God

Holy Relationships

Living in Love

September Love

Claiming Your Own Life

School Factory

Love, Infidelity, and Sexual Addiction

Gratitude Therapy

One Day At A Time

Learning To Be A Good Friend

Happy To Be Me

Worry, Worry, Go Away

God Made Us One By One

MD Hanley

MD Hanley has been a software engineer for over 30 years. He is passionate about technology and the way it constantly changes. He finds it to be a never-ending source of excitement and inspiration.

MD Hanley has always been an avid reader, and he developed a love of storytelling at a young age. His books include a financial thriller book called **Bit By Bit**, a cyberpunk thriller book called **Carbon Copy**, a science fiction book called **Quantum Mind**, and another book in the Spiritual Way of Life Series of books called, **Humility: A Spiritual Way of Life**.

MD Hanley is an adventurer at heart. He enjoys hobbies like scuba diving, flying, and hang gliding. His experiences flying through the congested New York controlled airspace, hang gliding off a mountain top, or scuba diving on the Great Barrier Reef have led to some interesting and unique insights into the world around him. MD Hanley is a talented software engineer, accomplished book designer, but also a gifted storyteller. He is passionate about technology, storytelling, and adventure. His work is sure to entertain and inspire readers of all ages.

Books by MD Hanley

Bit By Bit

Bit by Bit is a crime thriller about Gary McKeown, targeted for murder by his business partner after discovering his involvement in a bitcoin scam. Gary wakes up from a coma with no memory and embarks on a global chase to uncover the truth.

Carbon Copy

Carbon Copy is a cyberpunk thriller about a world where every disease can be cured and aging is nonexistent, one man holds the key to unlimited power. In the wrong hands, it could mean the end of humanity as we know it.

Quantum Mind

Quantum Mind is the second book in the **Quantum Genesis Series** is the story of twins, Kat and her twin brother Pat, who meet Alder who came to Earth over 5000 years ago. His ancient mission was to help planet Earth join a group of sentient planets quantumly connected around the universe. Does Alder complete his sacred mission?

Humility: A Spiritual Way of Life

The fourth book in the **Spirituality as a Way of Life Series** describes how Humility: A Spiritual Way of Life is a path of self-discovery. Humility helps to have a realistic sense of oneself, leading you to find the perfect balance of peace, confidence, and purpose in your life.

Spiritual Way of Life Series

If you liked **Joy: A Spiritual Way of Life,** you can also find five additional titles in the **Spiritual Way of Life Series** currently in your favorite bookstore.

Gratitude: A Spiritual Way of Life

Acceptance: A Spiritual Way of Life

Humility: A Spiritual Way of Life

Love: A Spiritual Way of Life

Peace: A Spiritual Way of Life

Go to

https://www.hanleyadamspublishing.com to

link to your favorite bookstore.

Thank you for reading **Joy: A Spiritual Way of Life**! We hope you enjoyed it as much as we enjoyed writing it. If you did, we would be grateful if you could take a moment to leave a review on the site where you bought this book, or if you want to go to https://www.goodreads.com and share any thoughts or information you would care to leave about this book. Reviews are incredibly helpful for authors and also help other readers discover new books.

Thank you for your support and happy reading!

Christine A. Adams

MD Hanley